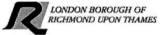

Richmond upon Thames Libraries

Renew online at www.richmond.gov.uk/libraries

Louise Spilsbury

W
FRANKLIN WATTS

Franklin Watts
First published in paperback in Great Britain in 2020 by
The Watts Publishing Group

Credits
Series Editors: Sarah Eason and Jennifer Sanderson
Series Designer: Emma DeBanks

Photo credits: Cover: Dreamstime: Alexandru Cuznetov (top); Shutterstock: TTStock (bottom); Inside: Dreamstime: Kelly Boreson 26c, Martin Brayley 10, Dtfoxfoto 20–21, 22, 26, Lukatdb 23, Stephen Mulcahey 6r, Shijianying 18, Dave Willman 8; Shutterstock: 1000 Words 7, 14c, David Alary 17, Arindambanerjee 6–7, Carl Ballou 14–15, Bibiphoto 5, P Cruciatti 9, Edw 22c, David Fowler 21b, Giovanni G 28, Fisun Ivan 25, Matej Kastelic 24, Julius Kielaitis 21t, Peter Kim 15, Liushengfilm 10–11, 16, Miamia 4–5, Pres Panayotov 27, Ramira 2, Savvapanf Photo 19, Howard Sayer 12–13, Smikeymikey1 1, 11.

Every attempt has been made to clear copyright. Should there be any inadvertent omission please apply to the publisher for rectification.

Dewey number: 363.2
ISBN: 978 1 4451 4508 2

Printed in China

Franklin Watts
An imprint of
Hachette Children's Group
Part of The Watts Publishing Group
Carmelite House
50 Victoria Embankment
London EC4Y 0DZ

An Hachette UK Company
www.hachette.co.uk

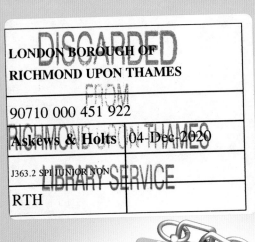

CONTENTS

SAVING LIVES

Who do people call when they are in difficulty or if there is an emergency? Police officers, search and rescue officers and lifeguards are just some of the people we turn to in times of need. Careers such as these are really important because the men and women who do these jobs save lives. People who choose this kind of career face serious challenges, difficulties and dangers. However, they also get a huge sense of satisfaction because they make a real difference in other people's lives.

The police officers that you see on the street spend their working lives solving crimes and helping people.

Challenging Roles

Police officers are the brave heroes and heroines who respond to emergencies, investigate crimes, keep the peace at public events and sports stadiums and much more. People who become police officers thrive on challenges and they are willing to work hard to learn the skills necessary for this difficult, but very important, job.

Police officers are the first to attend the scenes of many different crimes, including robberies.

A Career for You?

Here are some things to consider when you are thinking about which career is right for you:

- What are you good at? What are your interests, hobbies and skills?
- What kind of person are you? Do you prefer to work alone or do you like to work in a team or group? Do you think you would like to do physical work or would you prefer to work at a desk?
- Talk to your teachers or a **career advisor** and find out as much as you can about jobs that interest you. Reading this book is a good place to start.

HEROES ON THE STREET

Being a police officer is a tough and **unpredictable** job. Police officers are trained to help people in danger and they often have to put their own lives at risk to protect someone else. Police officers help the public in many different situations. They break up fights and chase **armed** criminals who are speeding from the scene of a crime in a stolen car. They patrol the streets to make citizens feel safe and they investigate crimes. Police officers are there to help others day and night, seven days a week. Being a police officer is a job that requires **dedication**, bravery and commitment.

It is the job of a police officer to deal with public disturbances such as cars that have been set on fire.

WHAT MAKES A GREAT POLICE OFFICER?

Many different kinds of people become police officers but they all share certain **characteristics**. These are personality features that make a person suited to this important and challenging job. A police officer must be:

- Responsible: police officers feel a need to help others and can always be relied on.
- Brave: police officers are willing to put themselves in danger to save others.
- **Empathetic**: police officers must be able to identify with, and be concerned about, other people's feelings and needs.

Which of the above do you think is most important and why?

Becoming a Police Officer

Police officers complete an **intensive** training programme before they start **patrolling** the streets. Local forces may have different criteria but all applicants must be 18 years of age and pass a series of written and physical tests. They must also undertake security checks to prove their identity and their background.

Police officers, and other emergency services, must be brave. They often deal with potentially dangerous situations.

A TYPICAL DAY

Police officers respond to thousands of calls each year. Although no two days are the same, this is what a day in the life of a uniformed police officer might look like.

A POLICE OFFICER'S DAY

- **7 am** Officers are briefed by the sergeant about assignments for the day, these may include ongoing problems they need to be aware of. They are also given areas to patrol.
- **7:30 am** Officers do **paperwork** from the previous day's **shift**. They also check **incidents** that have happened in their area since their last shift.
- **9 am** Officers start to patrol the streets in their area, by car or on foot.
- **10:30 am** Officers drive to the area where a home was broken into the night before to look out for an **offender** matching a **witness's** description. They also interview the neighbours.
- **2 pm** After lunch, officers continue their patrol. They also follow up a call about **vandals** damaging a park.
- **3 pm** Officers attend an accident scene where a car hit a truck. No one is hurt and vehicles are soon moving again.
- **4:45 pm** Back at the police station, officers finish the day's paperwork and prepare a report for the sergeant that lists ongoing incidents. When officers working the night shift take over, they will use the report to continue the investigations.

Police officers may patrol the streets during public gatherings such as festivals.

Police Officer Hours

Being a police officer is not a 9-to-5 job. Officers may start early and not finish until 10 pm, or they may work night shifts. An average day can be much more **hectic** than shown on page 8, because officers have to stop patrolling and follow up on every call that comes in on their radio.

EQUIPMENT

In order to perform their jobs **effectively** and keep themselves and others safe, police officers carry a variety of tools. Many of their tools are carried on their kit belt. The kit belt often holds a torch, a **baton**, pepper spray and handcuffs. Some officers also carry **tasers**. Batons are used to help **restrain** an offender and pepper spray irritates the eyes and nose. Officers use these tools to help them control **suspects**. They also wear a protective vest that acts as **body armour** to protect them from knife and gun attacks. Authorised Firearms Officers (AFO) are specially trained officers, who can carry **firearms**.

Police carry equipment on their kit belt around their waist so it is easy to get to. This leaves their hands free to do other things.

Using Technology

Officers are trained to use important technology, such as two-way radios and computer systems. Police cars have computers that are linked to the station. All police car computers are also connected to one another. The computers have instant messaging, so that officers can talk to one another through the radio. They also use the computers to gather information about suspects.

Officers may put the equipment in their kit belts in a different order, but they always keep the most important tools within easy reach.

handcuff

WHAT MAKES A GREAT POLICE OFFICER?

Officers on call must be ready to respond to any type of situation. They could be called out to search for a lost child, to stop a family argument that has become out of hand or to stop an armed robbery. Why do you think police officers have to be prepared, alert and ready to take in every detail of an incident at all times?

ON PATROL

Police officers on television are often shown in high-speed car chases with dangerous criminals. However, being a police officer is not just about excitement and adventure. Officers spend a lot of their time on patrol. They walk, cycle or drive around an area to check for signs of criminal activity. They also get to know local people and local problems. This helps **communities** feel safe.

Often, while on patrol, officers will be called to an incident in their area. The majority of the time these are community problems that the officer can solve without making an **arrest**. By listening to people and understanding their concerns, police officers can find workable solutions to minor issues like complaints about noisy neighbours or concerns about local thefts.

Police Community Support Officers (PCSOs) help the police deal with minor offences, advise local people and pass on information that helps the police solve crimes.

WHAT MAKES A GREAT POLICE OFFICER?

Police officers need good **communication** skills. They use these to form relationships and build connections with, and between, people and groups. Good officers are constantly in touch with the community they serve. How might having good relationships with the community help police officers find out about issues and solve them without needing to take people to court?

Patrolling on foot means that people can easily approach an officer to ask for help.

Caring for the Community

To patrol a neighbourhood effectively, police officers need to gain the trust of the community there. Officers spend time out of their cars, talking to residents and making contact with businesses and community leaders. They may also go to public meetings to discuss any issues that affect the neighbourhood.

INVESTIGATING CRIMES

An investigation begins as soon as someone calls the police about a crime. Police officers go to the scene of the crime and speak to the victims involved. They take details of what happened or what was stolen, if it was a robbery. They also take descriptions of what the offenders looked like.

Then, officers gather together and interview witnesses. They take photographs of the crime scene and watch any security footage available. Police officers may also call in a **scene of crime officer** (SOCO), who will take fingerprints and collect other types of **forensic evidence**. Officers close off the area where the crime happened. This stops evidence from being **contaminated**. At the end of the officers' shift, they enter the crime into the crime-recording system. Officers on the next shift then have all the evidence they need to continue the investigation.

Uniformed police officers are usually first at the scene of a crime such as a shop robbery and vandalism.

WHAT MAKES A GREAT POLICE OFFICER?

Great police officers work well with different types of officers, including counter terrorism units and **detectives** (see pages 24–25). They also work with other agencies, such as the fire department. Why do you think it is important for an officer to be able to work as part of a team and understand the importance of co-operating with others?

Learning the Law

Police officers are taught about different laws when they are training. When they become police officers, experts talk to them about new laws or changes to existing laws. They are also regularly given books with updated information about the law.

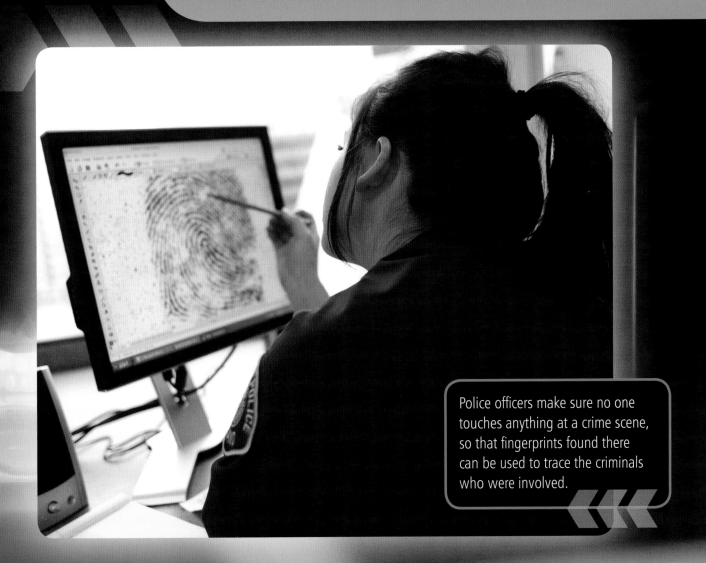

Police officers make sure no one touches anything at a crime scene, so that fingerprints found there can be used to trace the criminals who were involved.

D NOT CROSS

MAKING AN ARREST

At the end of an investigation, when evidence has been gathered and studied, and suspects have been interviewed, officers may feel they have enough **proof** to arrest a suspect.

When officers arrest a person that they believe has committed a crime, they have to explain to the suspect what his or her **rights** are. Officers may search the suspect for weapons, stolen goods or evidence of a crime. Next, the suspect is taken to the police station and booked. This is when officers record basic information about the suspect (such as his or her address and date of birth). Officers take the suspect's fingerprints and photograph him or her. After the arrest, police officers pass evidence and information about the crime to the **Crown Prosecution Service (CPS)**. The CPS decides what charges should be filed against the suspect in a **court trial**.

Police take a suspect's fingerprints and keep them on police records. The fingerprints may link a suspect to a crime scene.

Paperwork

Police work does not involve active duty alone. Police officers spend a lot of time completing paperwork. They have to write detailed reports and fill out a lot of forms. They must prepare cases and evidence for others to use during a case or for them to use themselves if they have to testify in court.

WHAT MAKES A GREAT POLICE OFFICER?

Good police officers are confident and **assertive**. When they try to arrest a suspect, he or she may resist, or fight, the arrest. Police officers must judge how best to take control of the situation and what action to take. How do you think speaking calmly and firmly, and behaving confidently, can help prevent a situation getting out of control?

WORKING WITH ANIMALS

Some police officers work closely with dogs or horses to enforce laws and catch criminals. Police dog handlers work with dogs trained for one particular job, such as sniffing out explosives, electronic devices or finding missing people. Together, handlers and their dogs patrol airports, ports and harbours. They also search prisons and vehicles. Dogs are trained to chase and catch suspects who try to escape police officers. Dog handlers must have complete control of their dogs at all times.

Police sniffer dogs can be trained to find illegal substances, such as drugs, at ports.

Mounted police officers help protect people in situations in which it would not be safe for officers to patrol on the ground. For example, they use their horses to control crowds or act as a barrier to threatening behaviour at sport events or demonstrations. Mounted police are also used for patrols and to take part in ceremonies.

Becoming a Police Dog Handler

Most dog handlers begin their careers as uniformed police officers. After two to five years of police work, they apply for a dog handler position. They then take part in a training programme with a dog partner. There are only a few jobs, so competition can be high.

Mounted police are police officers who patrol and carry out some police duties on horseback.

WHAT MAKES A GREAT POLICE OFFICER?

People who want to pursue a career as a mounted police officer or police dog handler need to have a real love for the animals in their care. They must exercise and care for the animals. Why do you think officers that work with animals also need to be very fit to do their job?

AFFIC POLICE

ic police are responsible for the safety of all motorists,
sts and **pedestrians**. They deal with a variety of
ents, such as vehicle crashes, injured pedestrians,
king that vehicles on the road meet safety rules
chasing stolen cars. They patrol streets and issue
 for offences.

 police are often called upon to go to the scene of a road traffic
nt. Officers are trained to manage the traffic when the road is
ed by an incident or accident. They examine the scene, interview
sses, provide basic **first aid** for any injured people until trained
medics arrive and take written **statements** from drivers and
sses. They may also have to clear any **obstructions**.

Driving Skills

Drivers of police traffic cars and motorcycles go out on patrol and
can be called to incidents. These officers may have to drive at high
speeds, so they are trained in advanced driving skills. These skills
help them drive quickly while keeping themselves, their passengers
and other road users safe.

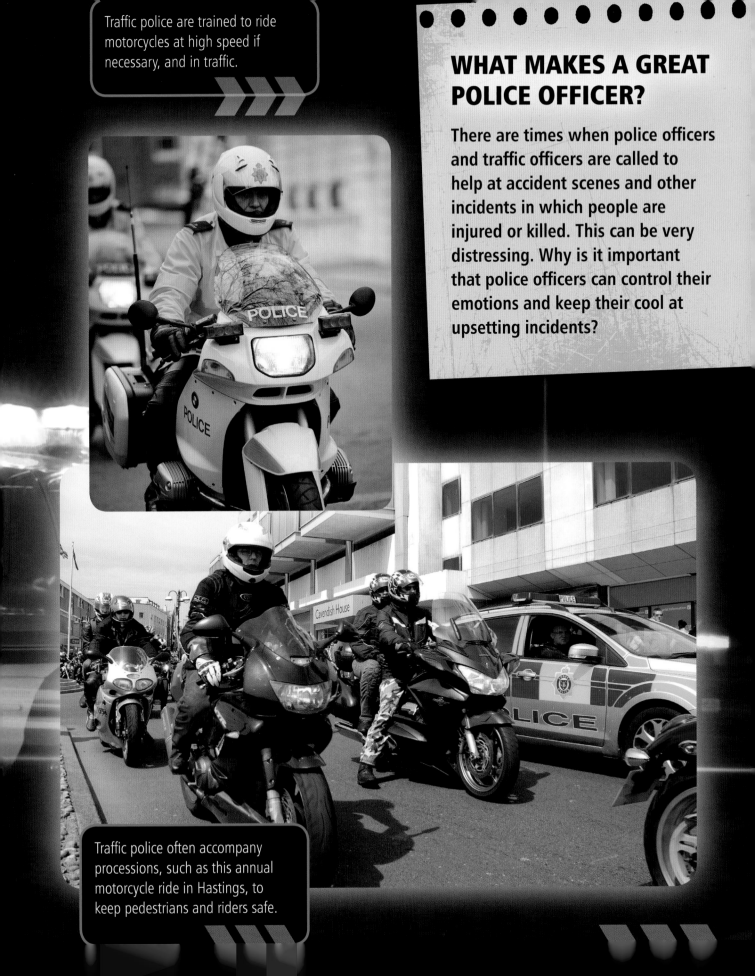

Traffic police are trained to ride motorcycles at high speed if necessary, and in traffic.

WHAT MAKES A GREAT POLICE OFFICER?

There are times when police officers and traffic officers are called to help at accident scenes and other incidents in which people are injured or killed. This can be very distressing. Why is it important that police officers can control their emotions and keep their cool at upsetting incidents?

Traffic police often accompany processions, such as this annual motorcycle ride in Hastings, to keep pedestrians and riders safe.

SCENE OF CRIME OFFICERS

SOCOs locate, record and **recover** evidence from crime scenes, such as stolen cars or a home that has been robbed. This evidence can be used to help solve crimes and **prosecute** suspects.

SOCOs work alongside uniformed and **plain-clothed** police officers during an investigation. They wear fully protective suits, so that things like their hair or clothing fibres are not left at a crime scene. They search for different types of evidence, from footprints and fingerprints to tools and weapons. They collect the evidence carefully so that it is not contaminated or damaged. They photograph, video or make notes about the crime scene. They send evidence to another department to be examined. For example, fingerprints are sent to the local fingerprint bureau, where experts examine them.

SOCOs check all surfaces for evidence, such as fingerprints or clothing fibres.

WHAT MAKES A GREAT POLICE OFFICER?

SOCOs need excellent **observation** skills. They must also be thorough and very patient. SOCOs may study the same crime scene for a long time, patiently working out what evidence there might be and seeing details that other people do not spot. How do you think paying attention to detail helps SOCOs collect important evidence?

SOCOs wear protective suits so that they do not contaminate the crime scene. They also photograph any evidence that they find.

Technology Training

SOCOs are trained to use special equipment to locate evidence such as fibres, hair and blood. Chemical powders will show up fingerprints and marks from shoes, and a special liquid will change colour if it comes into contact with blood. SOCOs also use special lights to show up the faintest of marks, which would otherwise go unnoticed.

23

DETECTIVES

Many crimes are solved by uniformed police officers. If a crime is serious or cannot be solved by patrol officers, detectives are given the case. Detectives are police officers who have been trained in investigative skills. They wear plain clothes and drive **unmarked cars**.

Detectives work with police officers, SOCOs and other experts to solve a case. They study physical evidence and interview suspects, witnesses and victims as they try to piece together what happened during an incident. They work on a case until it is solved or until they can go no further with the evidence. Detectives in large police forces often specialise in a particular type of crime such as murder, theft, missing persons or vehicle theft. This allows detectives to gain a huge amount of experience and knowledge in their crime area.

Detectives use and analyse evidence found by SOCOs to build a case against a suspect.

Becoming a Detective

To become a detective, you must undertake training to become a police officer, then complete two years as a uniformed officer. Selection for a post as a detective is very competitive. Many officers gain valuable experience working **on attachment** in the Criminal Investigation Department (CID), where detectives are based, before applying for the role.

WHAT MAKES A GREAT POLICE OFFICER?

Good detectives have great instincts, or gut feelings, about people
and evidence, but they also have strong **analytical** and people skills.
Detectives learn to read people's **body language**. For example,
sweating, chewing fingernails or turning red are all signs that
someone might be telling a lie. How might reading body language
help detectives find the truth when interviewing suspects?

RISKS AND REWARDS

Being a police officer has risks. It is a tough job with serious responsibilities and dangers. Police officers have to deal with angry, unpredictable people who may strike out or run away to avoid arrest. They must face oncoming, fast-moving vehicles when controlling traffic in an emergency. Sometimes, they may deal with armed criminals. However, with the proper training and equipment, most police officers enjoy a long and rewarding career.

The biggest reward for being a police officer is having a job that really counts. Every day when officers go to work, they are making life safer for people in the community. By doing so, they are making an area a better place to live. Police officers go home at the end of the day with a huge sense of achievement, knowing they have made a difference.

Continuous Training

Police officers are constantly training to keep themselves safe and to stay one step ahead of criminals. They train in different types of investigations, different computer databases and in self-defence and other policing skills. Being prepared helps officers to do their jobs.

WHAT MAKES A GREAT POLICE OFFICER?

Great police officers are brave and always willing to do the right thing, on or off duty. They will put their life on the line for someone they do not know. They really want to serve the public and their local community. Do you think you have similar personality traits? If you do, maybe you have what it takes to become a police officer.

It feels good to make a difference! Being a police officer is a very challenging job but one that also brings real rewards.

COULD YOU HAVE A CAREER AS A POLICE OFFICER?

Do you want to become a police officer? Following these steps will help you reach your goal.

School You do not need specific qualifications to become a police officer, but it is a good idea to join teams because teamwork is an important part of the job.

Volunteer Volunteering with your local police department is a great place to start. However, volunteering with any community service organisation can provide you with some of the skills needed to be a community police officer.

Keep fit Join school sports teams or find other ways to exercise regularly because police officers have to be fit.

Behave You must have a history of lawful conduct. You will need to pass a background check. Your past behaviour and the choices you have made must show positive traits that will support your application.

Tests You will have to pass a series of assessment tests, such as working with numbers, communication, reading and writing skills, handling information and decision making before being taken on as a trainee police officer. You will also have physical fitness and health checks.

Work Work experience prepares you for the long hours and strict rules that come with being a police officer. You do not have to do a job related to law enforcement, although that can help. Any work experience shows that you are responsible and capable of doing a job well.

Police training All police officers attend some form of police training, where they take physical and written exams before they can enter the police force.

GLOSSARY

analytical Being able to reason and solve problems.

armed Carrying a firearm or gun.

arrest To seize someone and take them into custody.

assertive Showing a confident and forceful personality.

baton A short stick.

body armour Clothing worn to protect people against stabbing or gunfire.

body language Gestures, facial expressions and body movements that give clues to how people are feeling.

career advisor A person trained to help people find out which career is best for them.

characteristics Features or qualities belonging to a particular person or thing.

communication The giving and receiving of information.

communities Groups of people living in the same place or who share common interests.

contaminated Spoiled and unusable.

court trial The place where both sides of a case for and against a criminal are heard.

dedication Devoted and completely committed to something.

detectives Police officers trained to investigate serious or complicated crimes.

effectively Doing something in a way that gets results.

empathetic Having the ability to share another person's feelings.

evidence Documents, witness reports and other information that can prove whether something is true or false.

firearm Rifle, pistol or other portable gun.

first aid Help given to a sick or injured person until full medical treatment is available.

forensic Scientific methods and techniques used to investigate crimes.

hectic Very busy.

incidents Accidents or dangerous events.

intensive Involving a lot of effort or work.

observation The act of careful watching and listening.

obstructions Things that are in the way.

offender Someone who has committed a crime.

on attachment To spend time with a different police department.

paperwork Forms, reports and other records that must be completed.

paramedics People who have medical training to deal with injured people at accident sites.

patrol Keep watch over an area.

pedestrians People walking.

plain-clothed Not wearing a uniform.

proof Something that shows that something else is true or correct.

prosecute To try to prove a case against someone accused of a crime.

recover To get something.

restrain To stop someone moving.

rights Legal entitlements to have or do something.

scene of crime officers (SOCOs) Police officers who locate, record and recover evidence from crime scenes.

shift A time period in which different groups of workers do the same jobs in relay.

statements Written or video recorded accounts of something that happened.

suspects People who are thought to be guilty of a crime.

taser A weapon that fires barbs that give an electric shock.

unmarked cars Police cars that do not have any markings to identify them.

unpredictable Behaving in a way that cannot be predicted or known.

vandals People who spoil or damage other people's property on purpose.

witness A person who sees something happen.

FURTHER READING

Police (Emergency 999)
Kathryn Walker, Wayland Books

Police Forensics (Radar)
Adam Sutherland, Wayland Books

Police Units (Edge)
Daniel Gilpin, Franklin Watts

Sniffer Dogs: How Dogs (and Their Noses) Save the World
Nancy Castaldo, Houghton Mifflin

WEBSITES

Read all about how police officers train, what they do and more at:
www.gmp.police.uk/content/section.html?readform&s=6B8B2141790C8CB8802579F E0046F1EA

Read more about a police officer's work at:
www.policecouldyou.co.uk/police-officer/what%27s-it-like-to-do-the-job/index.html

For career information about police officers see:
https://nationalcareersservice.direct.gov.uk/advice/planning/jobprofiles/Pages/ policeofficer.aspx

Read about a day in the life of a police officer at:
www.northumbria.police.uk/ebeat/myhub/beingacop/dayinthelife/index.asp

Note to parents and teachers
Every effort has been made by the Publisher to ensure that these websites contain no inappropriate or offensive material. However, because of the nature of the Internet, it is impossible to guarantee that the contents of these sites will not be altered. We strongly advise that Internet access is supervised by a responsible adult.

INDEX